DEVOTIONAL
GUIDE

Overcoming Conflict

Gloria Saddler-Reed, MDIV

WESTBOW
PRESS®
A DIVISION OF THOMAS NELSON
& ZONDERVAN

WestBow Press books may be ordered through booksellers or by contacting:

WestBow Press
A Division of Thomas Nelson & Zondervan
1663 Liberty Drive
Bloomington, IN 47403
www.westbowpress.com
1 (866) 928-1240

ISBN: 978-1-5127-2901-6 (sc)

Library of Congress Control Number: 2016901643

Print information available on the last page.

WestBow Press rev. date: 02/05/2016

ACKNOWLEDGEMENTS

****

During my seminary studies, I was faced with various oppositions and felt like giving up many times. I felt over whelmed with my studies and I just wanted to sit on the side lines and put the gifts and talents God had given me on the top shelf. So, I resolved in my own mind that I would just attend church, sit in the pews, listen to the Sermons and then go home.

But, upon taking a Managing Conflict course at seminary, I was encouraged to share what I had learned with others so that their faith in God could be strengthened like mine had been. I am so glad that I listened to my professor as this book would not have been written. Thank you, Dr. Scott Shaw who showed me that God is bigger than any problem or conflict and that when we rely on God's strength and not our own, we can overcome every hurdle.

INTRODUCTION

****

You are of God, little children, and have overcome
them: because greater is he that is in you, then he
that is in the world
1John 4:4

This *Devotional Guide* was written to help those who are struggling with various conflicts, whether in their own lives or someone they know who might need a little guidance, on how to biblically deal with conflict in their own lives. Sometimes, life can throw us such a curve that spins us out of control, but it is during these times that we need to know that there is someone we can rely on that is bigger and more powerful than our problems. Jesus said to cast all of our cares upon him because he cares about us (Matthew 11:28-30) and warns us not to become weighed down with the cares of this world, but to keep our focus on God and the building of His kingdom (Matthew 16:26, Matthew 6:33).

Before God called me to the ministry, I thought everyone in the church I attended was a Christian, especially the leaders. I would see people hugging each other and hear them say, "Praise the Lord" even those who didn't know me did the same to me. Everyone including the volunteers of the church made me feel at home by the kindness and warmth they showed me. I admired the pastor of the church who was more like a father to me who taught the word of God fluently and with great knowledge. I can honestly say that I was elated to be a part of such a big loving family.

One day I was sitting in the balcony of the church during one of the services when God called me to be a minister of the church. I went to the pastor and related this to him in which the pastor told me to call the person whom he had put in charge of the minister's training of the church and tell him that I had his (the pastor) seal of approval. After numerous phone calls and messages to that person, who incidentally never returned my calls, I contacted the pastor again to let him know what had transpired and to seek his advice on what my next steps should be. Again, I was told to contact the person and tell him that I had the pastor's seal of approval in which I did with no response. Finally, after much travailing and prayer, I was contacted for an interview to confirm if God had truly called me to the ministry! I didn't understand why I was going through this. I found myself consistently crying on the way home from my ministerial classes and I vowed within myself never to return after each class!

After much prayer and seeking the will of God for my life and the ministry God had called me to, I was able to continue the classes and God resolved those conflicts and gave me the strength to persevere. I realized like the apostle Paul that I could do all things through Christ, who strengthened me (Philippians 4:13). After completing my ministerial classes and being ordained as a minister of the church, I realized that the conflicts had come because God was pruning and honing me for something much bigger. God paved the way for me to finish Seminary and to receive the training I needed to become a hospital Chaplain.

I firmly believe that my studying what the word of God said and by applying it to the situation or conflicts I was experiencing in my life, I was able to overcome every hurdle and take some valuable learning with me along the way. Christians are encouraged to put on the whole armor of God so that we can withstand the evils that will come against us to weaken our faith (Ephesians 6:11). Thus, God dealt with me during my various conflicts and showed me that the word of God has a solution for every conflict known to man. God also made me realize that unlike modern day psychiatrists or psychoanalysts whose practice it is to observe human behavior in order to come up with a practical working hypothesis of how to guide the person through their immediate crisis until a firm solution can be found, God doesn't have to rationalize or theorize about man because God created man from the dust of the ground (Genesis 3:19), made man in God's own image (Genesis 1:26), formed man in the womb (Jeremiah 1:5) and has a working plan for man's life (Jeremiah 29:11). In Ecclesiastes 1:9, King Solomon affirmed that there was nothing new under the sun and that for every problem under the sun, the word of God offers solutions.

As you read this Devotional, Reflect on how the early Christians dealt with conflicts they encountered and how you too can look to God for the strength you need to persevere and endure hardships that may come your way. Use the **Reflection** section to write down your thoughts and your feelings and use the **Resolution** section to see how God's word can apply to the conflict(s) you may be experiencing in your life and what you can do to resolve these conflicts. Remember, God is Omnipotent (all power); Omniscient (all knowing); Omnipresent (everywhere at the same time) and that God's love for you will never end. God can do anything but fail so feel confident that God has your best interest at heart.

Conflict within Oneself

****

I find then a law, that, when I would do good,
evil is present with me.
Romans 7:21.

Christians face many adversities and have to make many moral decisions that will honor God and bring glory to Him. In our daily lives, we are faced with oppositions and temptations to follow others in their wrong doings just because it looks and feel like the popular thing to do.

Like the apostle Paul, we are in a constant struggle with our flesh to do or not to do those things that do not please God. This in itself can be very frustrating and tiring even for the seasoned Christian who has been a faithful follower of Christ for many years. But Paul reminds us that God is bigger than our struggles and that God will deliver us (**Romans 7:24-25**).

If it be so, our God whom we serve is able to deliver us
From the burning fiery furnace and he will deliver
us out of thine hand, O king.
Daniel 3:17

Reflection

Resolution

Moral Conflict

And be not conformed to this world, but be transformed by
the renewing of your mind, that you may prove what
is that good and acceptable, and perfect will of God.
Romans 12:2

Most young people today feel they are not having fun if they can't hang out with their peers who think that homosexuality, losing one's virginity, smoking pot, or having babies out of wedlock is cool, but they don't think of the ramifications that such loose living can have on the outcome of their future. While these struggles are real to all Christians and they certainly fit the 'signs of the times' in which we live, the apostle Paul reminds us that what God thinks about what we do or don't do is of the upmost importance.

Paul goes on to reminds us that in order to be pleasing to our heavenly Father, Christians are to *"present their body as a living sacrifice, holy, acceptable unto God, which is our reasonable service,"* Romans 12:1. Paul also lists a number of unrighteous acts in 1Corinthians 6:9-10 that if practiced, will certainly keep us from inheriting or getting into the kingdom of God. Therefore, the apostle Paul warns us not to be deceived by the lust of the world but to hold to what God says in His word and know that God's word is "truth" (John 17:17).

If you then be risen with Christ, seek those things which are above,
where Christ sits on the right hand of God. Set your affection on things above,
not on things on the earth.
Colossians 3:1-2

Reflection

Resolution

Victory In the Mist of Conflict

****

For I am now ready to be offered, and the time of my
departure is at hand. I have fought a good fight,
I have finished my course, I have kept the faith.
2Timothy 4:6-7

The apostle Paul faced many trails and temptations while preaching the gospel of Jesus Christ to the Gentiles (2Timothy 4:5) and was facing execution by the hands of Nero who was the Emperor of Rome at the time. Paul describes his evangelism of the gospel as a race in which he admonishes all Christians to train for so that they could run and cross the finish line.

According to the apostle Paul, we are to run life's race with diligence and perseverance while seeking Jesus' help so that we can gain the victory over every situation or adversity that may arise. We are to look to Jesus, who is the author and finisher of our faith and know that in and through Him all things are possible because He strengthens us (Hebrews 12:2; Philippians 4:13).

"These things have I spoken unto you, that in me you
might have peace. In the world you shall have tribulation;
but be of good cheer; I have overcome the world".
John 16:33

Reflection

Resolution

Conflicts with Those of like Faith

****

They departed asunder one from the other: and so Barnabas took
Mark and sailed unto Cyprus;
Acts 15:39b

Luke gives us a glimpse of how conflict of interest can cause division in Christian relationships as it did with the apostle Paul and Barnabas. Paul and Barnabas had shared many evangelical journeys together while preaching the gospel (v. 36), but became divided regarding one of the disciples whom Paul felt might desert them as he had done earlier in their ministry (v.38). Also, Barnabas wanted to go a different way than that of Paul.

Sometimes in our relationships with others we may fail in our efforts to see the other person's point of view, but when we embrace the gospel of Jesus Christ as our main objective as it was with Paul and Barnabas, we can put aside our own selfish motives and work together for the common good of others. Thus, the final analysis will be the continued and effective work of the ministry which will bring glory, honor and praise to our God and not unwanted attention to us.

For by one Spirit are we all baptized into one body,
whether we be Jews or Gentiles, whether we be slave or free;
and have been made to drink into one Spirit.
For the body is not one member, but many.
1Corinthians 12:13-14

Reflection

Resolution

Dealing with Adversity

****

Hear us O our God; for we are despised;
Turn their reproach upon their own head, and give
them for prey in the land of captivity:
Nehemiah 4:4

No matter how we try to walk upright before the Lord and try to treat others with love and respect, there will always be someone who will ridicule us for being different than them. Because of Nehemiah and the Jew's effort to restore the walls of the city in Jerusalem, Sandballat the governor of Samaria tried to use scare tactics to get them to stop because he wanted to claim the city for himself. The Jews met with many oppositions and unseen dangers by those from without who didn't want them for neighbors, but they did not become discouraged or quit. They held on to their faith in a God who had proven to them time and again that God was their refuge and strength and a very present help in times of trouble (Psalm 46:1). Thus the Jews finished building the walls of the city and built an altar to give thanks to God for all He had done for them (Nehemiah 12:27).

The Lord is my rock, and my fortress, and my deliverer;
my God, my strength, in whom I will trust; my buckler,
and the horn of my salvation, and my high tower.
Psalm 18:2

Reflection

Resolution

Overcoming Impatience

****

The discretion of a man deferreth his anger;
and it is his glory to pass over a transgression.
Proverbs 19:11

Jesus Christ had much to say to his disciples about overlooking others offences by encouraging them to look first at their own faults (Matthew 7:3-5). Sometimes we are quick to point out the faults of others, especially if we are the one who have been wronged, even to the point of breaking off the relationship. But Jesus reminds us that we are not perfect and that we too make mistakes. Jesus also encouraged His followers to be patient and kind to one another by looking within themselves before judging others. Most importantly, Jesus taught how we should forgive others freely just as God freely forgives us (Luke 6:37).

Ask yourself; is there someone who has wronged me whom I have not forgiven? If so, what can I do to make amends and renew the relationship? Sometimes, all that's needed is to let the other person know that they are appreciated and loved.

But thou O man of God, flee these things;
and follow after righteousness, godliness, faith,
love, patience, meekness.
1Timothy 6:11

Reflection

Resolution

Conflict in Life

****

And He arose, and rebuked the wind,
and said unto the sea, "peace, be still".
And the wind ceased, and there was a great calm.
Mark 4:39

Jesus' disciples were in a state of panic as the storm raged against their boat. They tried frantically to keep the boat from sinking and from being drowned in the sea. In the end, they knew that they had to call on Jesus who was sleeping quietly in the lower part of the boat (Mark 4:38). Jesus arose from His sleep, commanded the winds to stop, and all was well.

When the storms of life are raging in our marriages, in our finances, and in our families, we don't have to give up and throw in the towel or do something crazy like hurting the ones we love or commit suicide. We have to trust God that He knows how to deliver and save us out of any situation we may find ourselves in. Like the disciples, we have to call on Jesus in our difficult times and believe that he will calm our storms and speak peace to our lives.

Casting all of your care upon him;
For he careth for you.
1Peter 5:7

Reflection

Resolution

Conflict in Marriage

****

Husbands love your wives, even as
Christ also loved the church, and gave himself for it;
Ephesians 5:25

God performed the first marriage in the Garden of Eden by giving Eve to Adam as a helpmate or companion (Genesis 2:18). Sometimes, husbands can be unyielding when it comes to receiving suggestions from their wives, which can make their wives feel unloved, not needed, or unappreciated. At the same time, wives can be overbearing and non-submissive toward their husbands by not recognizing that God have put him in authority as head of the household, and therefore make decisions that can cause problems and unhappiness in the marriage farther down the road.

For this reason, the apostle Paul reminded the Christians of his day the order by which God have arranged the family by holding the husbands accountable to God for maintaining the family unit. Of course, wives contribute greatly to the family unit by offering sound and logical suggestions to their husbands on how certain matters can be dealt with that will enhance the continuity of the family as a whole. Since husbands and wives are a team and thus considered as one flesh in Christ, they are therefore commanded to love, cherish, and to respect one another while working together for one common good, to please God, their Creator. (Eph. 5:31-33).

And said, for this cause shall a man leave father
and mother, and shall cleave to his wife and they twain shall be one flesh.
Matthew 19:5

Reflection

Resolution

Congregational Conflicts

Now therefore you are no more strangers
and foreigners, but fellow citizens with the saints,
and of the household of God;
Ephesians 2:19

No one wants to attend a church where they do not feel welcomed or sit in a particular seat that someone else feels belong solely to them. Our motives for going to church should be to worship and give praise to God for all that He has done for us. The last thing we need is for someone to make us feel like we are strangers in God's house. Undoubtedly, this is a reality in our churches today and was a reality in the early church that the apostle Paul felt he needed to address.

Paul felt that he had to address this issue because it was causing a division in the church between both the Jews and the Gentiles. Paul had to let them know that God had chosen them both and have drawn them together in Him before the foundation of the world and that they are all God's children by Christ Jesus according to His good pleasure and according to His good will (Ephesians 1:4-4). Conflicts in the church can be solved with love, patience, and wisdom.

There is one body and one Spirit, even as you are called
in one hope of your calling; one Lord, one faith, one baptism,
one God and Father of all, who is above all, and through all and in you all.
Ephesians 4:4-6

Reflection

Resolution

_____

_____

_____

_____

_____

_____

_____

_____

_____

_____

_____

_____

_____

_____

_____

_____

_____

_____

_____

_____

_____

_____

_____

_____

_____

_____

_____

_____

_____

Resolving Conflicts with Love

****

Though I speak with the tongues of men and of angels,
And have not charity, I am become as sounding brass, or a tinkling cymbal.
1Corithians 13:1

We have all gotten angry at times when someone said or did something we didn't like or didn't agree with. Anger like happiness, is a part of who we are as human beings. There are however, two kinds of anger; *justifiable* anger *and unjustifiable* anger. *Justifiable* anger falls under the category of Jesus' throwing out the money changers and cleansing the Temple (Luke 19:45-46). *Unjustifiable* anger, according to Jesus, is anger that is directed at others without reason or cause, for which, says Jesus, they will be judged (Matthew 5:22).

Jesus tells us how we can resolve conflicts when someone wrongs us by going to that person in love bearing our gift of peace so that the person that have done evil to us may see the error of their ways and the pain they have caused. If they listen and repent for what they have done, we would have gained our brethren (Matthew 18:15-17). We must admit that it is not easy to forgive or ask forgiveness of someone who has wronged us or who has no intention on righting the wrong. But, if we clothe ourselves in love and mildness, maybe it will help the offender (s) to see the good in us which may prompt a change in them.

Beloved, let us love one another; for love is of God;
and everyone that loveth is born of God, and knowth God.
1John 4:7

Reflection

Resolution

_____

_____

_____

_____

_____

_____

_____

_____

_____

_____

_____

_____

_____

_____

_____

_____

_____

_____

_____

_____

_____

_____

_____

_____

_____

_____

_____

_____

_____

_____

_____

_____

_____

Help in Times of Conflict

****

I can do all things through Christ
which strengtheneth me.
Philippians 4:13

On his many missionary trips, the apostle Paul met with various trials and tribulations while preaching the gospel throughout Rome and the Middle Eastern world. There are at least fourteen books of the New Testament that attests to the many hardships and near death experiences that Paul suffered and endured. But whatever his trials, persecutions or hardships, we are told that Paul continued to push forward in Christ and thus victoriously conquered every hardship and overcame every obstacle.

As followers of Jesus Christ, we will face and are faced with many adversities, many trials, many temptations, and many hardships. Like the apostle Paul, we have to trust in God and keep our eyes on the risen Christ, knowing that our strength and our victories come from Him. Also, when we reflect back on our past afflictions and hardship and realize how God has brought us through them all, this gives us the confidence in knowing that no matter what the hardship or trial, God cares for us and will empower us and give us the wisdom we need to overcome them (1John 5:4).

Who is he that overcometh the world,
but he that believeth that Jesus is the Son of God?
1John 5:5

Reflection

Resolution

Christian Faith/World Views

****

But he answered and said," It is written, man shall not live
by bread alone, but by every word that proceedeth
out of the mouth of God."
Matthew 4:4

For forty days, Jesus was without food in the wilderness when the devil (known as Satan) told Jesus to turn stones into bread so that He would fulfill his hunger need. But, Jesus reminded Satan that it was more important to feed on the spiritual word of God than to fill one's self with physical pleasures.

This world is filled with many distractions and desires that can and have stumbled many Christians who do not find themselves consumed in the word of God. In our "anything goes" society, Jesus stresses to all Christians the importance of reading and meditating on God's word so that they will know the will of God and live a righteous life before Him. The apostle Paul said "Do not be conformed to this world, but be transformed by the renewing of your mind, that you may prove what is that good, acceptable, and perfect will of God," Romans 12:2.

And the world passeth away, and the lust thereof;
but he that doeth the will of God abideth forever,"
1 John 2:17

Reflection

Resolution

Communicating in a Non-Conflictual Way

****

Jesus said, "But let your communications be, Yea, yea; Nay, nay;
for whatsoever is more than these cometh of evil."
Matthew 5:37

When I was a child, my mother would quote the above Scripture constantly while standing firm on decisions she had to make regarding my brothers and I. She was unwavering in final decisions and because of her examples; I learned to be honest in my dealings with others. This is precisely the point Jesus teaches His disciples in the above Scripture.

As Christians, the apostle Paul admonishes us to be people of integrity, always speaking truth one to another (Ephesians 4:15). On the other hand, if we are caught lying, stretching the truth, or cheating, people are not apt to trust or believe us even when we are telling the truth. Hence, Jesus was the epitome of truth and grace (John 1:17) and spoke the truth of God's word to all He encountered and He taught His disciples to do the same by admonishing them to follow His example (John 12:26).

But speaking the truth in love,
may grow up into him in all things,
which is the head, even Christ.
Ephesians 4:15

Reflection

Resolution

Conquering Fear

****

For God hath not given us the spirit of fear;
but of power, and of love, and of a sound mind.
2 Timothy 1:7

The world can be a scary and dark place that house people who do not yet know Christ Jesus in the pardon of their sins. Violence, gang warfare, drug trafficking, suicide, and other societal ills are running rampant in our communities, neighborhoods, and in our schools. People are afraid to point out criminals who have committed crimes for fear of losing their lives or someone dear to them. But as Christians, we are called upon by the word of God to be a shining light for Jesus Christ in this dark world, ambassadors as it were of the gospel of truth and peace (Matthew 5: 14, 16).

As the Holy Spirit works in us to make us different inside and out, we are given the power by that same Spirit to make a difference in our work place by not being afraid to convey biblical truths to correct the errors of others. For this reason Paul could say, "You have not received the spirit of bondage again to fear; but you have received the Spirit of adoption, whereby we cry Abba Father," Romans 8:15.

And fear not them which kill the body, but are not able to kill the soul;
But rather fear him which is able to destroy both soul and body in hell.
Matthew 10:28

Reflection

_____
_____
_____
_____
_____
_____
_____
_____
_____
_____
_____
_____
_____
_____
_____
_____
_____
_____
_____
_____
_____
_____
_____
_____
_____
_____
_____
_____
_____
_____

Resolution

_____

_____

_____

_____

_____

_____

_____

_____

_____

_____

_____

_____

_____

_____

_____

_____

_____

_____

_____

_____

_____

_____

_____

_____

_____

_____

_____

_____

_____

_____

_____

_____

_____

Conflicts of Neutrality

****

Wisdom is the principle thing; therefore get wisdom; and
with all thy getting get understanding.
Proverbs 4:7

King David instructed Solomon, his son, in the ways of the Lord God and told him to be courageous and wise for David was old and nearing death and Solomon would become heir to his throne. David wanted Solomon to get off to a good start by telling him to seek the commandments and the insight from God so that he would be able to make wise choices and decisions that would greatly affect God's people.

In the first chapter of 2 Chronicles, we get a glimpse of Solomon's obedience to the words of his father David, his prayer to God and God's answers to his prayer. Solomon listened to David and sought God in his decisions to rule God's people and God richly blessed him (2 Chronicle 1:6-12). Later when Solomon was tested by two women who were fighting over a child, Solomon had to make a quick and wise decision that would determine the future outcome of the child and its true mother by not favoring one woman over the other. Thus, Solomon remained neutral and made the right choice (1 Kings 3:16-27) therefore bringing glory to God. When we are faced with what decisions or choices to make in life, we too should pray and ask God to grant us wisdom, guidance and spiritual understanding so that we are able to make the right choice that will bring glory and honor to God (Colossians 1:9-10).

"If any of you lack in wisdom, let him ask of God,
That giveth to all men liberally, and upbraideth not; and it will be given him.
James 1:5

Reflection

Resolution

_____

_____

_____

_____

_____

_____

_____

_____

_____

_____

_____

_____

_____

_____

_____

_____

_____

_____

_____

_____

_____

_____

_____

_____

_____

_____

_____

_____

_____

_____

_____

_____

Tradition vs Conflict

****

But when Peter was come to Antioch,
I withstood him to the face, because he was to be blamed.
Galatians 2:11

It was the tradition of the Jews not to eat or associate with the Gentiles, but this was not supposed to be the case among the Christian brethren. Paul rebuked Peter and his actions before all who were present and made it clear to them that Jesus died so that everyone who believes on Him through the word of God may be saved (John 3:16; Acts 16:31). Paul had denounced the divisive practices of Jews versus Gentiles (non-Jews) by the gospel of Jesus Christ and was very determined not to build again that division. Peter and others were trying to impose their Jewish tradition on the Gentiles and Paul had to remind them that what they were doing was wrong and that living by faith in Christ was more important (Galatians 2:14-21).

Sometimes we can be very stubborn when trying to impose our beliefs or tradition on others of like faith simply because we think it is the right thing to do. But the apostle Paul reminds us as followers of Christ to, "fulfill you my joy, that you be like-minded, having the same love, being of one accord, of one mind," Philippians 2:2.

Be of the same mind one toward another. Mind not high things,
but condescend to men of low estate. Be not wise in your own conceits.
Romans 12:16

Reflection

Resolution

Learning Humility through Conflict

****

"Whosoever therefore shall humble himself as this little child,
The same is greatest in the kingdom of heaven."
Matthew 18:4

Jesus' disciples were having a heated discussion one day about who would be greater in God's kingdom. Their argument became so heated that Jesus felt the need to use a little child in order to explain to them the importance of being humble. Jesus wanted them to see the importance of leaving behind their self-centeredness to become like that of a child in humbleness and sincerity of heart, which is the only way anyone can enter into the kingdom of heaven.

Jesus taught His disciples that pride was what caused Adam and eve to disobey God and thus brought the whole human race into captivity to sin and death. His valuable lesson also taught them and yet teaches us the key to entering God's kingdom; not by arrogance, force or social status, but by humbling ourselves under the mighty hand of God so that He can and will exalt us when the time is right (1 Peter 5:6).

There hath no temptation taken you but such as is common to man;
But God is faithful, who will not suffer you to be tempted above that ye are able;
but will with the temptation also make a way to escape, that you may be able to bear it.
1 Corinthians 10:13

Reflection

Resolution

Maintaining Peace

****

Blessed are the peacemakers,
for they shall be called the children of God.
Matthew 5:9

This is one of the many "Beatitudes" that Jesus quotes to his followers when teaching them that being at peace with all people is a blessing that will eventually lead to eternal life in God's kingdom. Many themes are woven into the gospel that Jesus gives and one of those themes have to do with peace which renders the gospel message also as the 'gospel of peace'. Like thread, peace is wove throughout Scripture and is to be one of the characteristics of a Christian's life in their walk with God.

When we look at all the injustice, unrest, violence, sorrow, pain and hardship that's around us, it becomes seemly difficult to find peace anywhere. Our leaders speak of peace and try to come up with ways to assimilate it in our countries, our states, our cities and even in our neighborhoods, but they are far from any real solution.

Whatever the situation in the world we live, we must constantly keep in mind the words of Jesus regarding the troubles His followers will have because of their faith in Him, but He promises to give us His peace so that we will be conquers and peacemakers in this world through His strength (John 15:18,16:33; Romans 8:37; Philippians 4:13).

Thou will keep him in perfect peace,
whose mind is stayed on thee: because he trusteth in thee.
Isaiah 26:3

Reflection

Resolution

Struggling with Aging

****

Those that be planted in the house of the Lord shall flourish in
the courts of our God. They shall still bring forth fruit in old age;
they shall be fat and flourishing.
Psalm 92:13-14

Some people look at growing old as a burden to be reckoned with by their children or those who have to care for them when they can no longer care for themselves. It is true that the older a person get the more effort it takes to get normal activities done on a daily basis. King Solomon gave a good example of the aging process and what all mankind will have to contend with as they lose their youthfulness in Ecclesiastes 12:1-7.

There is also encouragement in growing old especially the wisdom that is gained from various life experiences. This wisdom is seen in King Solomon himself in his old age towards the end of his life when he said that there was nothing new under the sun and that the conclusion of the matter is to fear God and keep His commandments for it is the whole duty of man (Ecclesiastes 1:9; 12:13). Solomon had lived a long and prosperous life and because of the wisdom God granted him (1 Kings 4:29) he was able to meet the challenges of life head on and impart that wisdom to others so that they in turn may use wisdom to gain victory in their own lives. Likewise, when older persons share their life's experiences with the youth of their generation, it's like passing down precious pearls that can be treasured for generations to come.

The glory of young men is their strength;
and the beauty of old men is the gray head.
Proverbs 20:29

Reflection

Resolution

_____

_____

_____

_____

_____

_____

_____

_____

_____

_____

_____

_____

_____

_____

_____

_____

_____

_____

_____

_____

_____

_____

_____

_____

_____

_____

_____

_____

_____

Dealing with Anger

****

Let all bitterness, and wrath, and anger, and clamour, and evil speaking,
be put away from you, with all malice; and be ye kind one to another, tenderhearted,
forgiving one another, even as God for Christ's sake hath forgiven you.
Ephesians 4:31-32

We have all become angry because someone did or said something to us that was unwarranted. Some of us have angered others, maybe intentional or unknowingly. We have all heard the saying, "I can forgive but I can't forget." Well, the apostle Paul is asking us to do just that when he tells us to put away the bitterness and the anger that destroys so many relationships, especially those of the body of Christ. This was the problem in the early churches in Asia among the Jewish and Gentile Christians which threatened to tear the church apart and divide Christians into two groups.

Paul had to write to these Christians to remind them that Christ died for the Church and that it was God who had united the two groups together in Him, Christ. Paul also had to remind and exhort them to make every effort to maintain the unity of the church which is one body in Christ (4:3, 4). Likewise, as Christians, we are to not only live in peace with all men (including those of the faith) but we are to show mutual respect to one another in and outside of the church, because our lives should always reflect that of Christ so that we might be pleasing to God (Romans 12:18; Ephesians 5:1-2). Jesus said that all would know that we are His disciples if we show love toward each other (John 13:35).

And above all these things put on charity, which
is the bond of perfectness.
Colossians 3:14.

Reflection

Resolution

Dealing with Bitterness

****

And the prayer of faith shall save the sick, and the Lord shall raise them up; and if he have committed sins, it shall be forgiven him.
James 5:15

A dear friend of mine told me some years ago that God was responsible for his wife's death. He was very angry with God and continued to drink heavily without regards to his own health. He had grown up as a Catholic and was an altar boy for most of his youth, but confided that he really didn't know the Bible, just what the priests wanted him to know.

I begin to minister to him about the love and forgiveness of God and the provisions He have provided for man through His Son Jesus Christ that heals the grieving hearts and saves the sin sick soul. My friend didn't want to hear any of this at that time but continued to hold to the fact that God was insensitive and unloving to let his wife suffer and die. One day he too became ill and the news he received from his doctor wasn't favorable. He stated that out of fear he began to pray, not just for healing, but for God's forgiveness for his sins and the anger he held onto because of his wife's death. God not only healed his physical illness but his spiritual ills were also healed because today my friend is free from alcoholism and is consistently seeking to live a life that is pleasing to God. He now believes that what happened to his late wife were the results of her years of smoking and physical neglect and not because God had executed His wrath and judgment upon her.

Bless the Lord, O my soul; and all that is within me, bless his holy name. Who forgives all thine iniquities; who health all thy diseases.
Psalm 103:1, 3.

Reflection

Resolution

Coping with Sorrow

****

He will swallow up death in victory; and the Lord God
will wipe away tears from off all faces; and the rebuke
of his people shall he take away from off the earth: for the Lord has spoken it.
Isaiah 25:8

We have all lost family members or those who were close to us. The sorrow and the emptiness that is felt from such loss can be devastating and even catastrophic. Some people have taken their own lives because they felt that they couldn't live on without their loved ones, especially the loss of a child.

By the power of God, the prophet Isaiah was granted insight into the future when God's Son, Jesus, would come into the world and put an end to the pain and suffering that death brings. The prophet was enabled to futuristically see the "Suffering Servant" (Jesus Christ) as he was beaten, bruised, ridiculed, despised and rejected before being put to death on the cross for mankind's iniquity (Isaiah 53:1-9). Through Isaiah's continual prophetic visions we not only get a glimpse of the sufferings and death of our Lord and Savior, we are also able to see his great victory for mankind over the power of sin and death for Isaiah tells us that *death will be swallowed up forever.* We must take pleasure in knowing that Jesus knows how we feel because his life here on earth was filled with sorrow and grief and as our eternal "High Priest" in heaven he is more than capable to bring us through (Hebrews 7:17-28).

O death, where is thy sting? O grave, where is thy victory
1Corinthians 15:55

Reflection

Resolution

Dealing with Negative Emotions

****

A soft answer turneth away wrath: but grievous
words stir up anger
Proverbs 15:1

It is not easy to forgive those who do wrong to us just because they feel that they can get away with it when they see that we are meek and especially when they know that we are confessed Christians. They are well versed in the cliché which says that *Christians should turn the other cheek* to those imposing the wrong. It is also easy to become bitter towards people like that which in turn causes one to harbor unwanted resentment or even hatred.

This is exactly what the apostle Paul is saying to the Christians at Ephesus, not to act like those that are without Christ but to imitate Him in all that we do and say. Paul's use of putting on and putting off is likened to that of changing clothes. We take off the old dirty ones and put on new fresh ones to start our day or to retire at night. In this same manner Paul exhorts believers to put away the old man which is our sinful desires of the flesh and to put on the new man, which is the new life wrought in Christ Jesus. This putting away includes getting rid of any bitterness, resentfulness and any hatred one might be holding against another so that we may put on kindness and tenderness in order to forgive one another as God in Christ has forgiven us (Ephesians 4:32).

And walk in love, as Christ also hath loved us,
and hath given himself for us an offering and a sacrifice to God...
Ephesians 5:2

67

Reflection

Resolution

Letting Go of Stinginess

****

Every man according as he purposed in his heart, so let him give;
not grudgingly, or of necessity: for God loveth a cheerful giver.
2 Corinthians 9:7

What type of giving does God like? The word 'cheerful' is taken from the Greek term *"hilaron"* from which the English term *"hilarious"* is derived. Although the word may suggest that one be cheerful, it is also a serious matter because God does not look at the quantity of the giver but at the quality and beauty of what a person gives.

When admonishing the Corinthians believers to give, Paul did not put any amount on their giving but entreats them to give freely from their hearts that which they are able to give. In other words, the amount of their gift or giving should be determined by God's call to give generously of their first fruits and not their leftovers. Paul also made them aware of the fact that God knows if one is giving out of love or because of feeling pressured to give.

Jesus knew the pleasures and the benefits of giving to others and admonished His followers to do the same (Luke 6:38). Also, God gladly gave His only begotten Son Jesus, who with great love willingly exchanged His sinless life for our sinful ones on the cross of shame (John 15:13; Hebrews 12:2). Thus, giving can be an enjoyable and delightful experience if the heart is rooted in love and unselfishness.

He that giveth unto the poor shall not lack;
But he that hideth his eyes shall have many a curse.
Proverb 28:27

Reflection

Resolution

Dealing with Discouragement

****

*Many are the afflictions of the righteous, but the Lord
delivers him from them all.*
Psalm 34: 19

The prophet Jeremiah was often discouraged when faced with the task of having to pronounce God's judgments to the backslidden faithless people of Israel. He was also known as the "weeping prophet' because he constantly wept over the sins of the people and the coming judgment that God was about to bring against them. The people did not want to listen to Jeremiah and tried numerous ways to stop him from prophesying so that they could continue to live the way they wanted. Thus, Jeremiah became so discouraged and frustrated that he vowed never to say another word to the people about God's judgment. But, Jeremiah 20:9 tells us that the prophet couldn't keep silent and continued to speak God's judgments in the midst of many hard trials.

Some times in the midst of life's struggles, we often become discouraged and frustrated when life doesn't go according to our plans or when we try to set right examples for those we love and they ignore or ridicule us and say things that hurt our feelings. Sometimes, because of our normal human feelings, we feel like giving up and decide not to help those who have hurt us. If Jesus had felt that way when he was being humiliated, beaten, and crucified on the cross for sinful mankind, we would all be lost without a Savior. Thank God Jesus' own feelings were nailed to the cross with our sins!

*These things I have spoken unto you, that in me ye might have peace.
In the world ye shall have tribulation: but be
of good cheer; I have overcome the world.*
John 16:33b

Reflection

Resolution

_____

_____

_____

_____

_____

_____

_____

_____

_____

_____

_____

_____

_____

_____

_____

_____

_____

_____

_____

_____

_____

_____

_____

_____

_____

_____

_____

_____

_____

_____

Bibliography

The Authorized King James Version Holy Bible. Thomas Nelson Inc. Nashville, Tennessee, 1987.

Printed in the United States
By Bookmasters